THE FOURTH PART OF THE WORLD

The Fourth Part
OF THE WORLD

David Weiss
1986 George Elliston Poetry Prize

Ohio State University Press   Columbus

Library of Congress Cataloging in Publication Data

Weiss, David, 1952-
    The fourth part of the world.

    I. Title. II. Title: 4th part of the world.
PS3573.E415F68   1986   811'.54   86-23466
ISBN 0-8142-0425-2
ISBN 0-8142-0426-0 (pbk.)

Table of Contents

Acknowledgments

Several of the poems in this book have appeared in other publications: "Cameo" in the *Antioch Review*, Vol. 40 (Fall 1982); "The Fountains," *Galileo Press*, Vol. 3 (Winter 1984); "On the Marshes at Dawn," *Georgia Review*, Winter 1980; "Hell's Kitchen," *Ironwood*, Vol. 11 (Spring 1983); "At the Cloisters," *The New Yorker*, 16 November 1981; "Against Prophecy," *Northern American Review*, Vol. 267 (September 1982); "Alders" and "Traveler's Advisory," *Partisan Review*, Vol. 50, No. 3; "Val-de-Grâce," *Partisan Review*, Vol. 52, No. 2; "Olive" and "Big Bang," *Ploughshares*, Vol. 10, No. 1; "In an Orchard on Thanksgiving," "This World," and "The Landlord," in *Poetry*, December 1981, January 1983, and February 1980, respectively; "Maine Carpenter," *Portland Review*, Vol. 28, No. 2; "The White Road" and "Heat Wave," *Prairie Schooner*, Winter 1984; "Starling" and "A Little Treasury of Love Poems," *Seneca Review*, Vol. 14. No. 1; and "This Sweet Thing," *Virginia Quarterly Review*, Vol 60 (1984).

Grateful acknowledgment is made for permission to reprint them here.

For Deborah

I

We say, "far away";
the Zulu have a sentence-word that means
"where one cries, 'Mother, I am lost.'"

—MARTIN BUBER

BIG BANG

As a boy I dreamed of striking out from earth
into the black unbreathable not-even-nothing

of outer space. As far as the awe of dreams
allowed, I went. The earth dropped away

like a turquoise ring into a bottomless lake.
I was terrified, I can tell you,

but keen for adventure. I kept on
until I came to a wall that went down

deeper than the Wailing Wall and stretched
wider than the Great Wall of China. There was

no scaling it. If anyone had known where I was
she would have yelled me home and whomped me one.

But with each hammer blow the red brick chipped away
and I fell through. Never had I been that excited.

There I discovered not the city of gold or a veiled
naked beauty or a bearded giant in purple robes

but more of the same senseless space that can't be
filled or comprehended or stared at for too long.

I woke then. To this day I am still awake,
trying to find the ring that slipped from my finger.

3

HELL'S KITCHEN

One looked on while the other
shoved the boy's face into the oily
concrete of the Hess station,
shouting each time he slammed it
down, *what did you call my mother?*
You could hear it happening,
but we were all boys. Already
it was too late for us. *Get off him,*
leave him alone, you're killing him,
I hollered, standing there, smelling
the Atlantic tide bully its way
up the Hudson, dying inside. But this
isn't about me or the caved-in
left side of his face. I lifted
him, after, out of his blood
and held him until he stood without
touching the ground. Then he looked up,
leaving my arms, and pirouetted
slowly like a blind figure skater
or a planet far from the sun.
And he said softly, *O my God, O*
my God, O my God, his arms spreading
wider as he turned. He was still
smiling when the two cops hurried him
into the back seat and sped off.
This was near dawn near Field's
bakery where two thousand loaves or so
of wheat and rye were rising, moist,

4

sweet, assured of delivery. I don't know
how long by the bread trucks outside
I took that in. But one greedy breath
at a time was all that was possible.

THIS WORLD

When I was sixteen
I couldn't get across
to anyone

that I wasn't meant
for this world
but a dimmer one

characterized
by evenly spaced blue lights,
continual rain,

women glimpsed
only in profile;
there, a familial stranger

kept to himself
listening
for an underground spring.

I would have called it
a way of life then,
not despair.

If someone had told me
that blood
in the veins of those

past help
yellows and runs watery
like urine,

I would have said,
sure, why not.
Nothing surprised me,

except cruelty.
Yet at this odd fact
heard the other day,

I shuddered
at how quickly
the charade is dropped.

Which is to say,
I now belong to this world
and can't recall

at which moment I realized
that to love
even the many shades

there are of lipstick
was no betrayal
but a respite

as if from
poorly tailored clothes.
I think of the elderly man

that brought us
beets and potatoes
whose roof in a force ten gale

blew off
like a paper hat.
Rocking in his chair,

he watched the stars
graze down
the black grasses to the west

and when his tea was cold
went to bed.
It was he I told

of meeting a woman
late one night in a bar.
As we left in heavy rain,

her make-up began to run.
I could see
that she was not just older,

she was sixty if a day.
But the hour and enough scotch
belittled such distinctions—

what did it matter?
Laughing,
we huddled close in a doorway.

It was then I saw
she wasn't a woman.
Spitting rouge and mascara,

he coaxed
in a deep, quivering voice,
don't worry, loverboy,

it'll be good, it'll be good,
while he fondled me
to the end.

I kicked him down the stairs,
blood
yellow in my veins.

The perfume he wore
lingered for days.
This friend,

who is now dead,
raised his teacup ceremonially
and said,

as representative, I welcome you,
you little bastard.
You're a member now in good standing

of the human race—though,
Lord knows,
we don't need any more like you.

THE LANDLORD

Shy of me, three niñas ride the elevator to the top floor.
I check the roof for leaks and find dead in the wet tar
a sparrow. Downstairs, mice run in the walls.
Like blood they skitter through the ear's hallways.
My father wakes in a language he doesn't understand.
He points the nose up and gives it more throttle.

Unexpectedly, this morning is my real homecoming.
Carlos hands a wrench to me under the sink in 6J
as the past turns away like a shoemaker shutting
the door, who goes back to his hammer and heel
as the ambulance speeds his partner away.
In the basement, the boiler clicks into infernal hymn.
Soot billows up like incense. In my hand, the brass trap
is cold, its weight undeniable. *Just like new,*
the shoemaker can't help admire when he's through.

What collects rent in the morning, gives heat in the evening,
doctors this torso of living brick and kissed a woman
in a dream at dawn? The elevator clanks, going down slow.
Carlos runs a hand through his little boy's hair, thinking—
what, Carlos? I listen for an acorn falling
to knock its helmet off on the forest floor.
Someone, late to pay, tells me *go to hell.*

Father, I am here but it's a riddle to me,
surprised at the stranger I've returned to be,
the one who walks on two legs at noon,
a troubled syllable cradled on his lips.
The sun strikes down this late September afternoon
as it did at Thebes
with all the elusive warmth of brightness.

SWING

That wintry spring I walked at Orchard Beach
driving from work to breathe the briny air
and air that shuttered room in which a boy
lay on his narrow bed tossing in a rhythm
for which I couldn't find words or pitch.
I'd tramp the boardwalk, the playground,
then out the jetty wondering if, instead,
I was meant to learn the greater intimacies of failing.

As I sat on a swing and pushed off
I imagined a woman next to me—
gaunt, gray-eyed, with wild, filthy,
silver hair, hugging a green jug:
I was an actress, a mother, I had it all,
she crowed, handing me the sweet wine.
And do you know why, do you know why?
I showed them just what they were feeling,
I could make them weep inside
for all their lost, lonely children.
That's right, I brought them right up out of Egypt.
But let me tell you something, she said
taking a swig, *for that glimpse of the promised land*
they hate your guts, and you know why?
Do you know what the promised land
looks like these days? she chortled.
I can see you're the romantic type. I pity
the woman whose son of a bitch you're going to be.

I had no other life to speak of then,
just the world of the see-saw, the slide,
the jungle gym, so I went when she did
to join beside a trashcan blazing up
four men sharing a stogy and a bottle
warming their hands and staring into
the easy inventiveness of the flames.
She laughed and whispered with each one,
but to me she said, *look at them mumbling,*
in love with rehearsing the past. Is that
the sort of poet you plan to be, my little man,
making lovely noises about love's bitter mysteries?

I listened to her talk all spring
as I pumped up into oak branches,
and back above the spiked iron fence,
swinging in a rhythm which turned
plunging into climbing into glimpsing
a wave breaking and, farther off, a ship.
Her voice went round and round like a life
preserver or a book among friends.
All spring as the oak made leaves
I could hear beyond the jetty
the bellbuoy clank its warning:
rocks, rocks, rocks, rocks.

THIS SWEET THING

One windless day in June
a maple leaf left the fold
and sank three prongs into my grandfather's skull.
They went in easily,
he was then already eight years in the grave.

He got up, it was his backyard.
I could tell he was confused.
He said, give me a hacksaw, Dave.
He said, christ almighty, what have you done to this place?
He said, well, I shat through a hole in my hip long enough.
Help me get this sweet thing out of my head
so I can be dead again.

But, for the love of God, we couldn't.

CAMEO

Who can say the world
won't be given back to us
more painfully than we imagine,

or that the afternoon
toward which she lifted her face
has already gathered in shadow.

This morning, that bird feeder,
the aperture in the trees
leading to water

all have in common a visitor
who could tell us more than we know
as if giving back

that portion of the painting
trimmed to accommodate
the only frame available.

What's to say
some jolt won't start
the clock on the mantle going,

or that the bathroom scale
doesn't already
register a small steady weight.

A cameo of afternoon light
smolders on the seat
of the chair as if

she was here
and rose
to singing just ahead.

Who can say that
a lie
is really a lie

or that this quiet isn't
in fact
a kind of choir in the trees.

A LITTLE TREASURY OF LOVE POEMS

Cornflower,
you don't know me from Adam.
I know you, I hope,
come June when you poke out
your trellissed blues,
shapely as Cygnus,
more faithful than the Seated Lady.

Before then, I can't tell you from Eve.

I've seen you beside highways most often
confined between shoulder and nearest tree
always stretching out ahead, disappearing.

Each time I step off into space,
you occur, odorless as sky,
and slip your arm through mine.

Then I wander your grove of Attic columns
toward some glistening yellowy altar
to receive like a word folded in a black wing

the blessing of pollination.

Did she know what she held, cornflower,
as enormous and silent in her arms
as the Andrea Doria going down?

She bent forward
as if it weighed infinitely more
than next to nothing.

It was beyond swallowing the warm blood
in its mouth, beyond
the least sound. Beyond her sudden love.

Up and back by the side of the road
she meandered,
like a vortex slowing down.

Who could you possibly keep from going under?

Did my parents ever know you
to climb into their eyes?

Did they never pull off the road
too angry to gaze down together
on some patchworked valley,

each to pour
a turbulent grief into your blue cup
that can hold nothing

but an undivided attention?
And later, hand in hand,
did they traipse through aisles of the feed corn below?

My love for them is not greater than it is for you.

Before you found my hard eyes,
I had wished to give my life
to a field of goldenrod, cracking

milkweed pods, rusted loosestrife.
Insects would have mounted my back
to mate

in the late, long shadows of the sun.

If you have something to do with corn,
I don't know what.
If you were a woman,
I could never look so long at you
without dropping my eyes,
pretending indifference.

19

But you are blind to all things
but the sun, common as dirt.
Whoever looks at you
finds his own troubles
sailing into view like winged seeds.

STARLING

It's extremely hard to track
one starling
in a flock of starlings.

I fixed on one
pecking in a muddy field
but lost him

as they all rose up
shuddering
to make in the drear day

a night sky, starry,
revolving on a secret point of air.
I lost another,

a blurry-winged Betelgeuse,
forgetting that I was watching,
daydreaming instead.

And again, moving forward,
when I stubbed my foot
on a lofty furrow.

Finally, I had one,
on a tether as if,
a plump meteor

blackly blazing,
a sign, a portent
of nothing in particular

to which I held on
for dear life, yes,
for that.

Hunger
or something less explicable
kept them spinning

in a thinned ring.
Dizziness
brought me to my knees.

And the stars fell,
burnt-out,
to feed around me

among stalks and soft clods,
even the least visible of constellations
near at hand.

II

Returning to himself, let man consider what he is
in comparison with all existence; let him regard himself
as lost in this remote corner of nature; and from
the little cell in which he finds himself lodged,
I mean the universe, let him estimate at their true value
the earth, kingdoms, cities, and himself.

—PASCAL

MIDWINTER SPRING

The earth was soft for December,
taciturn.
I sank at each step beside
dandelions
that had come back from the dead
of winter to chance
their brief, wholehearted lives.

I was out to pay my respects
to an oak tree
I knew how to stand before,
upright.

I had just hurt a friend I love
and didn't mind.
I had been walked on, I felt.
I had some pride.

Better, though, is to walk
beside grape vines
joined by wire, and gather
shrivelled grapes
that some picker missed
daydreaming
or while his back ached.

It is better to give off
a small, yellow
gleam, if possible, even
beneath snow.

Near dusk I came to
my solitary trunk which stood
squarely against the sky:
woodpecked,
honeycombed, squirrelled
with hickory nuts,
not a root intact, not
a limb to snap.

Together we listened
to a freight train approaching,
to brown, scrawny birds
twittering, that dived
on the bare vines and soared
back up empty
or with grape seeds on their tongues.

I looked down
into florets of blue-eyed
grass which gleamed
crowning the wrong season
undismayed.
I took it in.
I took in all I could,
then I struck out for home.

for Alan Meerow

WHITE ROAD

When the moon climbs up tonight
out of Seneca Lake, there is
always the off-chance she will plunge
back under its generous waters
without so much as a sound.

Here a fisherman reeling in, once,
hooked a swollen fist. As it surfaced,
he could see it clasped thoughtfully
to its other wrist, also severed,
the nails painted a bright red.

Of that poor she he dreamed for weeks,
and none too nicely.
I needn't tell you that.
Saints we're not.
Dive down to see what lies in bearded state,

and you may not come back . . .
With luck, the moon like a dolphin
will lift you as she climbs up.
Even now she is up paving
a white road over the water

on which we have all set out
at one time or another. I cup
its beginning in my hands
like a magnolia blossom
already bruising at my touch.

27

IN A BEEKEEPER'S WOODS BEFORE DAYBREAK

Some forty yards off: nine white headstones.
Mother, father, and all that comes of it.

I press my ear to the nearest one, and oh!
in my skull hums the industry of daughters.

I have come out searching for two lost dogs
and find myself wishing for a life
so faithful, so brief, it may never end.

They are fanning their wings,
these ten or twenty thousand bees,
and are to me as the Incan stairway
through the Andes, each a step.

I have come among them
breathing heavily, yelling my head off.
They are making heat out of honey.

Sisters, do you hear me in there?
I cannot rub my wings so rapidly,
though I have ears to listen.

Three below by the mercury . . .

Which of you will come through
only to die pollen-heavy and threadbare
beneath white and yellow wildflowers?

Which of you will work beside me
in the garden in May?

AT THE CLOISTERS

This is the herb garden of Bonnefont
shipped stone by stone and rejoined at this sun-
rich southwest corner to other medieval ideas
of solitude. No monk walks these paths between

quince trees and planted beds that radiate
from the marble wellhead in concentric squares.
I am turned aside, almost back, turning four times
four until stopped at the thick southern wall, gazing out.

Waxwings and starlings thrash the crab apple
trees swallowing whole fruits carnivally or
pecking them for seeds. Beyond, westward,
as each oak leaf in a slow drizzle of leaves

gives way to the austere pigments of ecstasy,
more of the Hudson comes into view like something
being unburied or an idea growing clearer.
Gulls sail the river with the ease of thought.

Joy in wilderness, peace in things tended.
I am pleased to be here among strewing herbs
and herbs for dyeing: mugwort and throatwort,
eglantine, thyme and celestial dill.

The fruitless pear disciplined to shape
holds its guided cruciform gracefully.
A Japanese couple kneels, better to see
the yellow nub at the heart of a snapdragon.

Starlings, en masse, rise and wind around the tower
like a vine or second hand. The bell tolls four:
time audible and time visible in a garden that
artfully squares off the infinite—devotion that undoes

dilemma. Cleverly the ripened quince spread a tart,
appley canopy of odor, solid as stone. I look down
to see the sky reflecting off the river—empty,
incomparable, bewildering were it not fleshed in

by the swan song of foliage on the Jersey palisade.
An act of love or sad miracle, a monk might ask as he
faced this watery tapestry of parts impossibly woven,
knowing that only the labor of his eyes held it together.

THE CONFEDERATE GRAVEYARD IN FRANKLIN, TENN.

Even in life
they represented
a great, posthumous idea.
For that, a General Hood,
"lion-hearted" and "wood-headed,"
saw fit to pass over
their less exceptional futures
and look approvingly out
on their charging and falling bodies.
Each minute
for five hours that afternoon
twenty young men lost out
on wealth/misery/happiness/etc.
Together they were adding up to something.

These are the same maples reddening,
grown large. Their fallen leaves
sough prolifically, shin-deep,
as we wade through the iron gate
whose half-hinged invitation
extends indifferently to
comings and goings alike: ours,
the brown thrasher's, and on
the evening breeze, the astonished
voices of unbodied men.

We read across the rows
and down as in a ledger book
leather-bound and crumbling.
In each column, the bottom line
roughly chiseled reads 1864—
1843-1864, common dates,
subtraction barely in the red.
This is biography condensed to a dash,
except where two recruits
share a headstone,
lying together, inseparable.

When we hear grunting and shouts
and feet running for all they're worth,
the ball I pick up isn't
musket or cannon but, yellow
in the deep, green grass, a tennis.
I throw it back across the road
to young men, confederated
in white, who represent a quieter,
no less posthumous idea
of the good life, measured easily
by pocket calculator
or the sweet, heavy air
that riffles a skirt of crepe
de chine pinned on a line,

which later at dusk will billow
musically about slender white ankles
in a soldier's mouldering dream.

In front of us the maple trees are burning,
a conflagration: shame, glory,
ardor, indistinguishable pigments
of letting go—if not tomorrow,
the day after. Eleven thousand suns
have set since this ground was turned,
tamped down; some must have smoldered
like this one warming our faces
as we bend close to a stone
and trace the crude lineaments
of a name that stands for nothing
more, nothing else.

for Rosanna Warren

TRAVELER'S ADVISORY

In the sun-backed cirrus
unfurling across the lake like rice paper,
your steady hand at work,
Kai Yu Hsu:

a robed traveler and the mountain
that towers above him
which he will climb alone toward evening
as shadows thatch his face.

I cannot make it out more clearly than that—
the traveler listens at the brook and prepares,
even as the mountainside turns ashen in the sky.
About his bare calves dimness like a vine winds indelibly.

A word, Kai Yu Hsu, before you start up the slender trail:
the hill of mud which poured through the walls
and snuffed out your pipe, filling your mouth,
has made you unimaginable to me; therefore,

when you hear the traveler's shadow glide past
toward the bamboo footbridge and the falls,
wish a word with him about the trail further up,
lay down the quills you have carefully

been shaving and step outside to hail him
and ask. He, in turn, will talk so surely of

the mountain's hard contours beneath moss
and mist and trees that he will unlatch the gate

and you will continue on in his stead.
Later, done working, he will hold up his hands
to dry like two smooth sheaves on which lines
merge and cross, verge and move off;

they will take his lifetime to translate.
All this while the traveler has been climbing:
above the treeline, above the clouds.
Now he is scaling the peak and soon will

have found the simple means to become
its pinnacle, erect, shadowless, his throat
enshrined by minerals and moonlight, his hand,
his sight, his incomprehension quietly eroding.

THE FOUNTAINS

> Even if it were true,
> Even if I were dead and buried in Verona,
> I believe I would come out and wash my face
> In the chill spring.
> —JAMES WRIGHT

This morning the fountains of Verona
send their waters up, unperturbed.
And sunlight, if not time itself,
passing through these clear steady jets
slows, as a man might slow
in a woman's body, refracting earthward.

In a dusty square the stalls
fill with cucumbers and melon
that will warm by mid-afternoon
almost to the seeds.
Even unsold squid won't mask
those lush pastel odors.

Quietly in the noisy heat of day
a man leans on a fountain
and passes the warmth of his hands
into rough curving stone.
Then a voice he loves calls him,
and he turns away.

Across the river outside the gates
they stroll until they cannot hear
the cleaver greet the wood block.
Simplified, they stop
where a vineyard and a graveyard
share a crumbling wall.

HUNTERS IN THE SNOW

   after Breughel

It must be a shock
to emerge from the unframed life of the woods
and see at a single glance the broad, ice-green sky
and, far off,

jagged mountains more vertically massive
than in the mind's enlarging eye—
it must take their breath away
until the squat, brick bell-tower of the village

sheltered beneath those peaks
leads the eye down
and back, spire
by snow-topped spire, to their own orderly town;

and to hear, all at once, shouts of children skating
and the fire
roaring outside the Inn of the Stag:
that, too, must alter their breathing,

quicken it or slow it down,
I can't tell which by watching them;
they don't pause to take it in, these three men.
It may be there's no dividing line for them

between where they have been and where
they are bound, between songs

39

they hum and hymns they sing.
A black bird with red and yellow markings on its wings

soars from a tree into open space as the earth falls away.
But they don't appear to notice this either.
The rising fall of their chests
scarcely changes as, hugging the ground, they descend.

III

And all my sour-sweet days
I will lament and love.

—GEORGE HERBERT

THE FOURTH PART OF THE WORLD

1

VAL-DE-GRACE

Where could I find you if not here?
Among faces chipped and worn away
I have looked everywhere for a likeness
that might mend a cleft tongue, a broken wheel.

> Such a little is enough for one.
> For two: little short of living stone
> and a staircase spiraling down.

If already you've kissed me in a drop of rain
or as I drew near turned from me,
I cannot tell. Shadows of too many columns
obscure what has become of me, of you.

> Corrugated tin caps the gilded dome.
> The iron gates of Val-de-Grâce swing open
> to close to open again.

Louis as a boy laid the first stone.
Later, soldiers lay in rows, infected, maimed.
Are the rights of man still much the same?
Stop jabbering, speak plainly, I can hear

you say. I don't even know your real name
or why I am pleading like this,
but OK—

What I want is a home you'll visit often, even
in my absence like rain through rotted roofbeams.
In the hallway of painful ends we will cry out for
and curse one another assured of some further descent.

That's my offer. Take it or let me alone:
a love which passeth understanding,
we can gnaw each other to the bone.

I'll be at the fountain off Rue Val-de-Grâce.
A footpath of sky through the chestnut trees
will lead you to me, to them—four maidens drenched
to the skin who buckle each night shouldering

the world. You can hear them praying, *let it be
done*. Yet in the morning, somehow,
they've raised it back up again.

2

OLIVE

Between a rock and a hard place
I lay down
and let the sea do its worst.

Waves trumpeted.
Spray shot up in a whirlwind.

Far from the tree I had fallen
and like bladderwrack lay
thinking only of you

who knows what to do with love
besides work it into flesh.

The tide rode in to drag me
you alone guessed how far under
before it tossed me back.

Shriveled, blackened, salty,
I lay dead to the world,

alive. I could taste what I had become.
And I spit. I spit,
and I praised the sea.

3

A GREAT HORNED OWL

I

I took you for something else
in the sky at dusk: a simple blackness—

crow, perhaps, or a burn on the retina.
But, no. On a telephone pole you lit

and caught me in the cattails
with an eye that knew me better than myself.

Only my human size kept us apart.
Feline, single-minded,

you lit off stropping day into night.

II

All night I lay in the tall grass
dizzy with your swooping.

All you wanted was a life.
All I wanted was a life of my own

among the cries of love,
of fright.

So both of us were vexed
and made fierce shrieks

that were not word yet,
not yet song.

III

A jackrabbit jumped,
and talons tore the sky

blue, red edged.
Shadow of a shadow,

I turned up my throat
to see the love

that was lost between us
go down.

IV

All day I wondered,
how small is the body

that breathes inside its feathers
like a man hiding in weeds?

How tough the heart gone blind in sunlight?

4

GOING DOWN

Who has not wished for your quick corruscating
clarity and got the slow march into snowy
mountains, each step up sinking deeper,
the going slower, steeper, snow blinding
the sun and lovers of the sun? Later, a clear,
frigid night and fires flaring across the valley

as solitary as that game we played: a glimpse,
an icy touch, and nothing more of you than
a twig snapping and leaves swirling at my knees;
then the seeking which lead me to a young buck,
whose ribcage, hollow as a bowl, brimmed over with
rainwater and blood, its fur alive to the touch.

As I stared, black birds sailed down and drank.
They made a sound I heard as: *drink.*
You were everywhere, substantial as air,
this snowy air. The deer's eyes glowed orange,
as filled with understanding as the sky,
and, like a leaf, I let go and made my bow.

Since then I have called you sister, fountain
of life, the pit, and now, my silhouette,
as everpresent and encircling as the horizon line.
At your snowy impasse I have paused a long time
before going down into that lush, blighted valley
that was once a land of good, once a land of plenty.

5

ALDERS

It is blue, the snow,
and colder than any name
you ever called me. My Balalaika.
My Bloodless One. *A blue*
which seems to seep from the earth,
from beneath your frozen eyelids.

The sun perches in the stiff young alders,
puffs out its blond feathers against this cold
we could have breathed back to life
like that titmouse in the matchbox.
But you won't turn your face to me.

When twilight deepens, I will
go out to keep the alders from dissolving
in the dark. I'll touch each one.
I began my life by touching you.
Soon your life began.

Now if I say, it is blue, the snow,
I mean there is nothing
that is not snow, nothing
that is not blue as your lips.

You had asked me to stay during your illness,
offered to pay.

No one can keep me that cheaply,
beautiful boy.

Tomorrow they will shut you in for good.
The sun will come up anyway.
They will lower you down inside me,
a constant dusk, gentian.
There, too, will you turn your face away.

I am going out soon to walk among the alders.
All I shall feel, as always, is myself
reaching out a stiff hand, myself
filling the air around each slim sapling.

I will arch over beside them
in wind that brings fresh snow
and drag my forehead on the ground.
For you. My disfigured one. My kouros.

IV

Oh life! 'tis now that I do feel the latent horror
of thee! but 'tis not me! that horror's out of me!
and with the soft feeling of the human in me, yet
will I try to fight ye, ye grim, phantom futures!
Stand by me, hold me, bind me, O ye blessed influences!

—HERMAN MELVILLE

ON THE MARSHES AT DAWN

This is a prayer
unspoken as the sowing of seeds,

crossing great emptiness
like a wedge of geese splitting the dark air,

offered like the shirt on my back
to a memory of trouble, to no one, to one other.

I am praying only for what's imaginable,
for an intimate, unreachable thing

that each day seems a footstep
further away, harder to get to.

But I say *wheat*
and a breeze bends it over or soon will.

I say *geese*
and already some are nesting in the cattails.

I say these words
and, like that, you are among them,

emerging as if from shadows
of laurel and stout cedars

as the world, drawing new breath
in the blueness of dawn,

holds it, briefly,
before the day-long sigh.

IN AN ORCHARD ON THANKSGIVING

We walked out among the spurs of the apple trees,
mending our lives behind with our life ahead.

Moonlight lit the frost that stiffened the field.
A brook spoke for us mixing milky metallic sounds.

We picked the last apple off a tree, shared its white
neglected sweetness, laughing over nothing at all.

A sparrow hawk swooped past your face,
then the sparrow hawk's shadow.

AGAINST PROPHECY

Tonight my wife turns to the wall troubled by death.
I say silly, joking things that do not comfort her
and go out closing the door and darkness in.

Rain drums down as it has for days.
I watch it run to the tips of palm leaves
where the drops pause to gather mass before falling.

Since we, too, pause, before falling, to gather mass,
the idea of not-being repels my wife's imagination
with its nothing-to-imagine—worse than the thought of being

buried alive. There is comfort in words like *millenium*
    and *messiah*
spoken last night by three rabbis in Jerusalem: news was
each dreamed the same dream that the end of the world was near.

I heard this while scraping spots of red and green paint
from the formica top of a desk purchased secondhand.
I felt, then, a need to love or defend the useless attention

I was giving to make its shabby surface uniformly white again.
Indifferent to prophecy, the refrigerator drones in the dark
like a common prayer; it keeps milk fresh—a principle by

which we abide as surely as we do the return of sunlight.
My wife is sleeping when I slip into bed, her eyelids
scratching the pillow secretly like a leaf trembling

in a breeze so slight that if you wet a finger
and held it in the air, still you could not tell
which direction it was coming from.

HEAT WAVE

> And remember carefully:
> only water and it alone
> everywhere and always stays true to it-
> self
> —JOSEPH BRODSKY

Sleep's hard in this heat. More water than air
is in the atmosphere, yet our hope is rain.
Thunder stammers the windowpane. We vibrate
sympathetically like two good strings on
a warped autoharp. The regal oak outside,
which dropped anchor when this hill was
pastureland, throws back its head praising
a breeze. The sky opens dropping good news
on its leaves but soon snaps shut again.

Tonight a book's sole good is making a breeze.
A line in this one goes, "If anything's to be
praised, it's most likely how/the west wind becomes
the east wind." At best, we're barely ourselves—
we could be tossing on the bed of an inland sea:
arms gone dorsal, time fluid as seawater
and all desire cleansed, skipping by the brain
straight into strike or scuttle, no greed or gods
or public good to explain it away. As the fan-book
says, "Let the murderer be a murderer, not a sage."

Sleep's hard when you want it. The heat takes
your breath away as if someone who resembles you

were squeezing your ribcage—there's no
squeezing back. In a dream you'll attack and wake,
shocked at whom you've hurt. Imagine how cool
the western seas were. No one fished them.
Teeth were for tearing then, and not meant
to help the tongue articulate the letter "t."
We'll touch, but later tonight. Belly-up we lie
blinking at the ceiling's choppy surface and let
the fan's current float us toward the rapids.

Whether we once slapped up on a beach,
or the sea drew back stranding us, no matter.
We have brought the bottom up with us.
Now our moist lungs are hooked on the same air
that seems dead set this evening on bringing
back the deluvian. No hope in that.
Our chests rise and fall like civilizations,
heaving our shortcomings chronically into
the present. That's to say, I often forget
you are here, at this moment, beside me.

This heat's a plague, a sign of blindness
no blindness will put an end to.
Relief, when it comes, simply will.
We'll feel it as a chill along our spines
when the robins stirring near dawn
give the light a song by which to see.
We'll shiver and roll closer as if into
a single, human shape with birds piping
around our heads. Their singing will mean
more than just another day's begun.

LEAVES, BRANCHES

> Nov. 13th . . . Yellow butterflies still.
>
> —THOREAU

1. Daybreak

The oak shook down, and we woke all last month
in stark intensifying light. By degrees,
it beautified my wife. Oak twigs
were leading which pieced together sky.
But I felt found out, asked what I hadn't
answers for. Chickadees took soundings each day.

Sunrise: grain stands straightest in the trees.
Water in the pipes pushed isometrically.
The brown trout in the upper pond all moor
easterly into the feeding stream.
Washing, this cold water seems clearest.
Maybe it's the knuckles' ache that's so
reassuring, so still life.

The steeple bell rolls its first Rs
as I go outside. Someone I'll never see,
who also roused dreamily and splashed
his face, milks the worn rope, sound pouring
purely down. Arriving here, it resembles
that small blond boy who finally found
his way through the woods.

He had trailed a doe in, squirming under
the wire. He wanted to touch her, stroke
her soft flank, her throat—a yearning
in the fingertips he'll feel elsewhere.
He couldn't get closer than a stone's throw.
After, he heard nothing but his own,
tiring steps. I found him by the pond,
prodding a red eft squirming in his hands.
It's so helpless, how does it survive,
who looks after it? he asked. *Why*
are there black rings around the red spots?
Later I daubed mercurochrome on
his scratched face and drove him home.

2. Morning

On a boulder, a squirrel is warming his belly.
As I come toward him, he starts up on all fours:
mica in the stone beneath darts and trembles.

A red fox on the path to the lower pond
has eyed me for days. Maggots work
its tenement body, dismantling almost all.
The real fox is long gone, having slipped
away while its throat was torn. Did she,
whom I also loved, escape with a similar
clairvoyance before the train tore the throat
of her stalled car? Time lights on hurt,
lays eggs in its eyeless place.
It comes to smell the same, although something
slips away like the water which spills over
to fill the lower pond—a far bigger one,
swimmable, clogged with algae. Frogs love it
for hiding, as do the neighbor's girls
who wade in knee-deep and catch them
more than half the time.

There's an urgency to days converging
from all sides as if to a point, the better
for driving in these pine fence staves.
From a neighboring spruce a crow sends

out its throaty self in threes.
The sledge sends back a steady, hollow
ring. Call and slow response. Yet
I'd rather be those two cabbage moths
spiraling up a post of sunlight,
tumble and flutter, effortlessly attuned,
as if discipline or love were at play.
Working the home stretch to the barn,
I wish my eight-pounder had wings,
this field fewer rocks.

3. Afternoon

A Boston man had owned this house,
a banker who summered here at first
and had the meadow plowed, edibles put in.
Each year until he died, after his handyman
retired, the garden shrank in size.
At the last, three years back, he set
a single tomato plant by the barn that went
unpicked, though his wife stayed on.
From that small patch we have salted slices
and put up three quarts of tomato sauce.
Although we'll replant in the spring
a prodigious yield will seem less bountiful, somehow.

On a rooftop the weathercock spins
lustily, looking . . . where, where?
Yet the few leaves on the many trees
don't stir, the wind surging as far
overhead as you are from me. Scraping paint,
painting trim, fence stringing, we've passed
all day at a distance which sets love astir
on its dried stem. From across the field
I shouted, out of hearing, and waved my arms
in a gust of feeling, helpless as an egg,
while you were planting bulbs. Then a hawk screeched
(a red-tailed hawk, I found its picture later)
and broke from a pinetop into the field
between us. Our eyes closed on those broad,

embracing wings and joined at the gray mouse
in its talons, docile, for the first time,
ascending. When I clutch you that surely,
are you no more attainable?

4. Evening

Up close, she's all equilateral triangles,
turning brown where she touches the ground.
I am down on my knees for this beauty,
this clumsy flier. Down here where small things
are large, the mantis lifts up and turns
like a master at t'ai ch'i and, simply,
goes off. In her meadow, the mare also knows,
although she's indifferent, swishing,
grinding grass. She tells time by the size
of her teeth. Soft sun, chilly wind.
It's me the seasons surprise, coming on,
coming on.

I know better what's built than what grows.
Standing off the road, I've learned to hear
wind from water from caterwauling,
to know what's the garbage truck far off,
and a tanager at a glance, like that
male in the silver birch, twin of sunset
off windowglass. Is it hello or goodbye?
Who's going, you or I?

Red blotches have emerged in the maple's
yellow like an unexpected desire: frigid
weather. They whirligig down to do slow
pirouettes on the pond's surface. The trout
below don't pay any mind, attent
only to inaudibles and invisibles.

At the pond's edge I stop. Keened,
nocturnal eyes watch you illumined in
the kitchen window. All around me,
soft calls and fierce cries.
So it's strange to see, as a leaf
touches down, an image of man
and dusky maple roar into syllables
of dark and light. When the tree
again branches on the pond more
leaves and my likeness will be gone.

MAINE CARPENTER

He said, we won't see apples on the trees again.
We bet on it. A bushel to the winner.
And no one to pick them or frame a house or fry eggs.
We put a skillet and keg of nails on that one.
Then it was love we got to, the last loss,
though he thought it might be first to go,
and as he lived alone, believing that in subtraction
lies the truth, I placed my wife in the kitty—
just then I was on the side of love, that underdog,
and he was lonely and late November drawing on,
and we had once believed in, perhaps only in,
ourselves. But he said, you keep your wife,
much as I like her. It's apples I'll miss,
and what's love to the bite of one almost too green?
I taste it, and I'm nothing else,
too much on the side of apples to predict things,
more than willing to be wrong. So I kept her
as we sat talking, too much on her side
for love to matter much. Your predictions,
I said, are just the heads of nails
shined up from walking on; it's the shining
grabs your attention. We said good evening,
and I went home crossing the wooden footbridge
which creaked and shifted, held fast by thousands
of nails hammered in before my time. I trusted
to them although some have loosened with rust.

Whoever lumbers over when one too many's worked
free won't be surprised. We live prepared
for it to feel familiar: the sudden let-go,
the freedom, then the soft mud and the pain
that comes, stopped by stone.

IN THE LUXEMBOURG GARDENS

We slipped in past the guards, I don't know how.
The gates were latched, the sprinklers shut down,
all the strollers gone. An orange canvas was
pulled over the merry-go-round where the ponies drowse.

It was a beautiful evening, and we will soon disappear
without a trace. In the catacomb of chestnut trees,
we drank from a plum, a nectarine, then glided
to the fountain the dead queens all face stonily.

In its blue-white flowering jet, we frothed over.
Ripples on the pond effaced our portraits:
already, then, you were growing weightless—
a boy ran a brass ring through with a wooden pike

and chortled; his pony galloped; your silk skirt fell away
to become a shape in the dirt a streetlamp made through
iron bars: an unappeasable cry announced the founding of
the state and soon will take our place in the shadows.

Our secret is: trespass lightly, spilling over,
and then go on. The French police are all but blind.
The gardens are closed, they inform us regretfully,
thinking we want in. We go. Separate ways

together. For an instant, turning back, it looks
like home—a huge, vacant lot fenced in.
For an instant I can still taste plum on your lips
and feel, inside us, the wooden pony rearing up.

70

IN FOG

Fog in the pine trees and the pasture.
Under our feet a cushion of sweet needles crackles—
three of us on four legs walking, an easy riddle.

A stallion trots toward us through knee-deep fog
and whinnies catching the scent of mare, and whinnies:
something draws close without drawing near.

In a gatepost crack you stroke a caterpillar's quilted bed,
and imagine its sleep and the end of sleep:
a fluttering up, awake. Inside you,

the wings are packed with care.
Their flexing and flying up are what we feel
startled to see a white-tail leaping over fences of air.

Here's a sadder riddle: what lives to die and dies of love?
Not the bullfrogs that bellyflop in as we skirt the pond,
or the goslings which panic the reeds they hide among.

We peer in the icehouse that once stored slabs of ice
shipped to the Orient to cool an emperor's wrists. Now
armchairs, umbrellas and antimacassars melt from mildew,

remains of the family that keeps the wider world at bay,
these woods a sanctuary, as you are for me, a vast enclosure
which protects the orange pilgrim flower, deer, birds of prey.

A puddle of fog brightens the path back;
we wade in and down and go under.
Out of sight, we stop to feel beyond our limits.

What dies to live outside its metes and bounds?
No riddle. We merge the smaller puddles of ourselves.
You grow dear to me, dearer than myself.

MACULATE CONCEPTIONS

> Let the period of the messenger cease.
> It is the time of the speaker.
> —POLYNESIAN CREATION MYTH

1

Nearly twelve weeks formed, we heard the heart
beat two strokes/second in your belly
mounding up like the tumulus at Newgrange.
Is it perverse to imagine you a burial chamber
where the dead put on new flesh, recollecting?
Or to imagine that a beggarwoman or luckless
thief who sneaked in from the cold might
kick again and squint its eyes at the sun
of the winter solstice trumpeting in?

2

Marina, Ezekiel, Frances, Fergus, Bernard.
We think up names that are umbilical cords.
Poor beginner! who will have to learn
how long ago in earnest he began
before coming to himself
naked and half-willing in a stranger's hands.

We name you in the hope that you'll be
among the ones who start a fire in their souls,
to whom the chilled, the troubled,
the more than old come to warm their hands
and whisper throwing shadows on the ground.

3

A half year from now with a wild shout
our he or she will be shoved out
into empty space
where the rough scratchings of urge and infinity
will carefully be traced and retraced
as lines on the forehead and on the face.

4

Penelope, Sarah, Adam, Saul.
Slowly orbiting soft inches from my cheek
at the crux of you, fully-made yet vague,
a rough sketch: eyes sealed, fingers unimprinted
with those aboriginal crosshatchings and swirls
I've seen depict two souls welcoming
an arrival to their island. Our newcomer
will soon discover that this cabbage patch
is no less strange than the isle of the dead
and that the best of our lot thrive
on dying of some sort.

5

I press my ear close
and hear nothing but your belly's gurglings.
What's going on where the never-before is being made
in that garden which goes to seed
at the animation of clay?

Is it only the dead or is it
we made less original by living
who yearn to be a bee in a cowslip's bell,
sucking the warm watery darkness,
dreaming of the hunt and the strike and the kill?

6

All those others she won't turn out to be!
Among them a girl I was a boy to years ago
who closed the distance between us
too fast for worn tires on a slick road,
closing all troubling distance altogether.

I will love our child as I loved her
when she died: freely, without stint,
unencumbered by personality.
Not without regret, however, and hurt, still,
by the curls which fell carelessly from her head.

With enough years, she will become herself,
and no generic word like lips or curl or hair
will do her justice—that grief behind all grief.

7

Forty pence we paid to be let in the gate
and climbed a stony hill to the bee-hive huts.
This night, dank and cold, recalls those flat, broad slabs
seven feet in length lapped round and up and in
on the Dingle peninsula by rough, agile men
a millenia ago that still take the roof-leveling wind
bred off the Atlantic and let in not a draft or drop.
We crawled in on hands and knees and stood in the dark
under its low dome shivering while the wind moaned outside.
I thought myself back into sheepskin and the shepherd's life
huddled against a hard gale that blew
long before Christ lay down for his three days dead.
I was like the howl which made its home in my ears:
unabandoned, affirmed, consoled by a wild fear.
And when the storm I conjured let up, we crept out
into a blue, blustery day that gathered in our faces
like sheep herded together for summer shearing.
Coming down we saw them baffled and chilly and unadorned,
standing alone, all bone and skin as our infant will be,
exposed to the air, shorn of all natural protection.

8

I have turned thirty-two today.
A child is on the way.
My hair is half-black, half-gray.
The wind on the lake is making waves,

a flat recitation of the daily round:
the pulling back, the rising, the crashing down,
a tireless obsessing that makes pebbles round,
that takes a thighbone or a thought and pounds

the shore until a perfect fit
is found, then pounds it
more. I'd have been appalled by that,
once. An infant takes its mother's teat

and sucks it dry. He burps then
sleeps, wakes hungry for more and
pumps, pulls. Not enough milk, and
he'll feel wronged, like hell, abandoned,

yet that, too, has its pleasures.
He wails extra loud, and his anger
helps explore his untuned powers.
Shutting his eyes, years later, he'll conjure

up a perfect wave that crests unbreaking.
It won't belong to any scene
he knows. Yet one day he will feel it breaking
naturally in his thoughts, sweeping

them along in its foam
that will grind them down
to size for the wind to take and float along,
it won't matter where. Alone,

he'll go, and no blessing will save
him. A father is someone in the way
and then he is the wave
itself, drawing back, completely gray

and powerful and gone, buried too deeply
to return a smile or give replies.
Six months from now, I still won't know why
the wind blows in gusts or suddenly dies,

or why pigments in the hair change.
I have never been much good with reason or with rhyme.
But I shall be the father of someone who washes up
amid sharp cries—his own and yours and mine.